Andrew Woods
Grace Romano

Oxford Grammar

Third Edition

Name: ______________________

Class: ______________________

1

OXFORD
UNIVERSITY PRESS

Contents

Topic 5: Text cohesion and language devices

Topic 6: Sentences and punctuation

Topic 7: Using grammar in texts

Topic 8: Extension and enrichment

Learning intention

We are learning to use nouns, plural nouns, proper nouns and pronouns in our writing to name people, places and things.

Unit 1.1 What is a noun?

The name game

1 Draw lines to match each picture with a name.

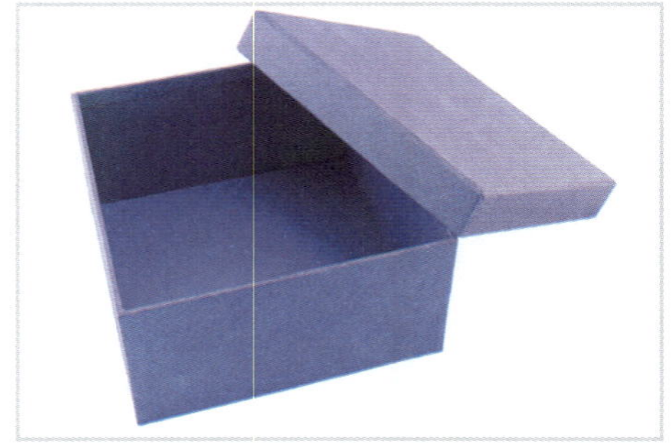

book
dog
Sun
box
pin
bag
tap
shop

Some words name things.

2 Circle the best naming word to match each picture.

dig dog

cup sip

bag carry

ship shut

tree try

ball kick

fox fix

flap flag

Try it out!

Draw pictures and write the **names** of five things you could see on a farm.

The Monsters' pets

Here are the Monsters.

Sami

Em

Trang

Cara

Ali

Max

Here are the Monsters' pets.

ant

dog

duck

cat

spider

pony

Some words **name** things.

Legs, ***wings***, ***pets***, ***bag***, ***cup*** and ***car*** are all names of things.

Read with your teacher.

The words we use for people, places and things are **naming** words.

1 Draw lines on the opposite page to match the Monsters' **names** with their pets.

- **a** Trang likes pets with six legs.
- **b** Sami likes pets with feathers.
- **c** Ali likes pets with eight legs.
- **d** Max likes pets that say, "Meow!"
- **e** Em likes pets that she can ride on.
- **f** Cara likes pets that can bark.

2 Which **naming words** can be pets? Tick them.

a puppy ______	**b** hill ______	**c** bird ______
d cup ______	**e** shop ______	**f** bag ______
g rabbit ______	**h** mouse ______	**i** kitten ______
j fish ______	**k** water ______	**l** door ______
m lizard ______	**n** key ______	**o** car ______
p apple ______	**q** lock ______	**r** horse ______
s lamb ______	**t** jelly ______	**u** paper ______

Try it out!

Can you write the **names** of three more animals that can be pets?

____

The Monsters at the beach

Naming words are used for people, places, animals and things.
Naming words are called nouns.

Look at the picture of the Monsters at the beach.

1 Tick the nouns (naming words) that you can see in the picture.

a girl ____	**b** house ____	**c** crab ____
d baker ____	**e** sand ____	**f** horse ____
g hat ____	**h** jetty ____	**i** frog ____
j lifesaver ____	**k** island ____	**l** ship ____
m pirate ____	**n** cubby ____	**o** fish ____
p dog ____	**q** sea ____	**r** flag ____
s tree ____	**t** farmyard ____	**u** Sun ____
v bat ____	**w** sky ____	**x** foot ____

2 Write four nouns (naming words) for things that you can see in the picture which are not in the list above.

____ ____

____ ____

Try it out!

Which word in this list does not belong?

crab bird fish run dog frog

Can you say why it does not belong?

____

Pip and Gog

When there is more than one person, place, animal or thing, the word for it can change.

What differences can you see between the two monsters below?

Here is Monster Pip.

Here is Monster Gog.

We can **add *s*** to some naming words to show more than one.
For example: *one hat – many hats, one dog – many dogs*

1 Add **s** to the naming words to fill the gaps.

a Pip has one eye but Gog has many ______________________ .

b Pip has one horn but Gog has nine ______________________ .

c Pip has one leg but Gog has several ______________________ .

d Pip has one mouth but Gog has a few ______________________ .

e Pip has one arm but Gog has four ______________________ .

2 Make these words more than one by adding **s**.

a head___ b ear___ c wing___

d toe___ e finger___ f monster___

g trunk___ h hand___ i eye___

Try it out!

Instead of just adding **s**, there can be other ways to show more than one.

Circle the best answer.

a Pip has one foot and Gog has four (foots / feet).

b Pip has one tooth but Gog has many (tooths / teeth).

c There are five (mans / men) in the team.

d How many (children / childs) are there in your class?

The Monsters' photo album

Some words are special names for people. ***Cara***, ***Max***, ***Trang***, ***Sami***, ***Em*** and ***Ali*** are special names.

1 Write the special names of the Monsters under their photos on the opposite page.

Cara has a ball.

Max has a book.

Trang has a flower.

Sami has an apple.

Em has a flag.

Ali has a balloon.

Special names for people, places and things start with a capital letter.

Some words are special names for places. ***Melbourne***, ***Sydney***, ***Australia***, ***Queensland*** and ***Uluru*** are special names for places.

2 Add special names to fill in this form about you.

Your first name: ____________________

Your last name: ____________________

The name of your suburb: ____________________

A friend's name: ____________________

Your pet's name: ____________________

Try it out!

Can you write:

a a boy's name beginning with A? ____________________

b a girl's name beginning with T? ____________________

c a place that begins with S? ____________________

Monster Town

Here is a map of Monster Town where the Monsters live.

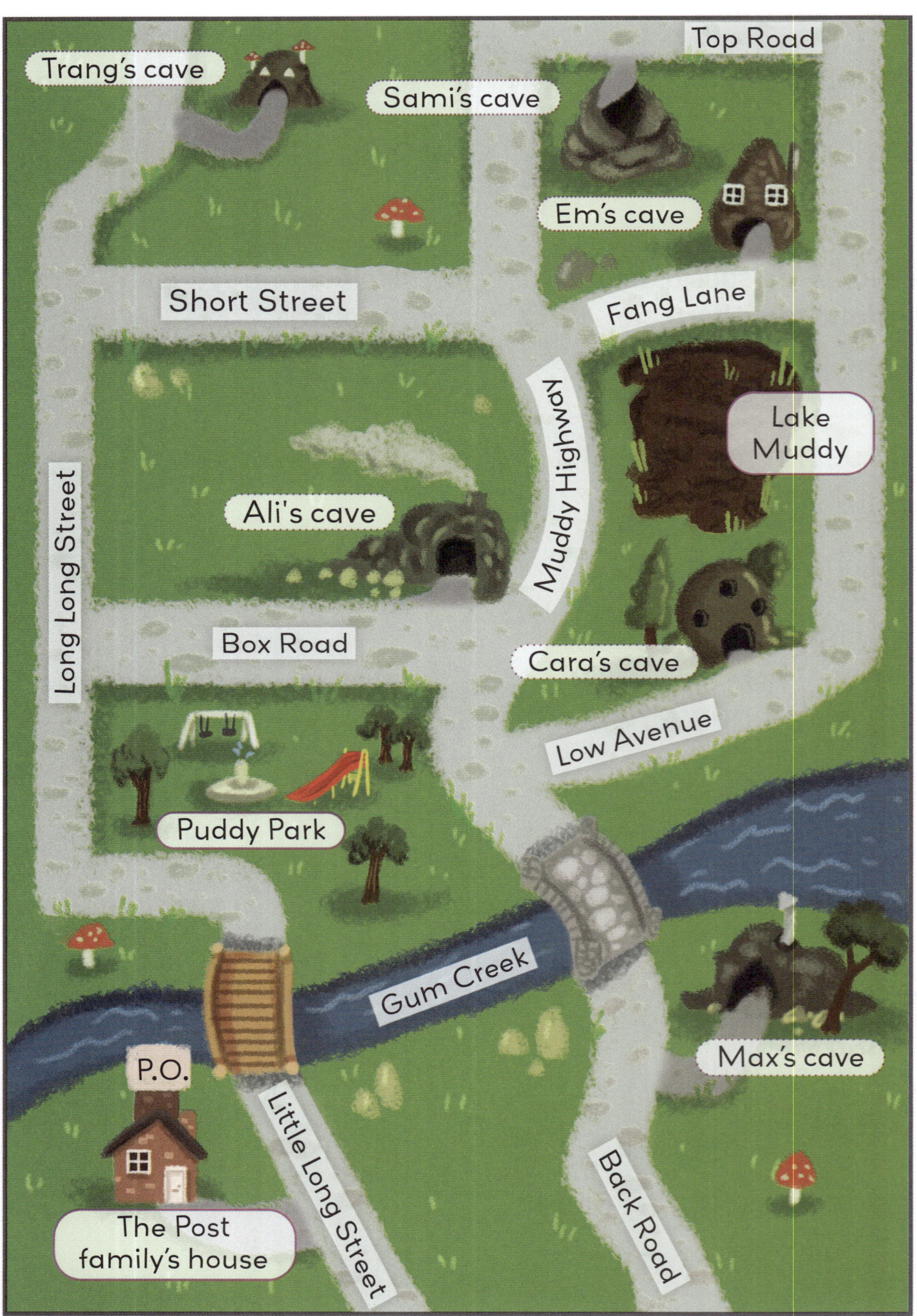

Some words are special names for people and places.
Australia, ***Paul***, ***Carlo*** and ***Linh*** are special names.

1 Look at the map to see where the Monsters live.

a Trang lives in ______________________ Street.

b Em lives in ______________________ Lane.

c Sami lives in ______________________ Road.

d Cara lives in ________________ Avenue.

e Ali lives on the corner of ______________
Road and ________________ Highway.

2 Who do you think lives at this address?

____

3 What is the special name of:

a Monster Town's lake? ________________

b Monster Town's park? ________________

c Monster Town's creek? ________________

4 On the map, colour the special name of the street where the Post family lives.

Did you remember that special names must begin with a capital letter? Special names are called **proper nouns**. As well as proper nouns, we have **common nouns**. These are the general names of things. For example, *city* is a **common noun**. *Sydney* is a proper noun. Sydney is the **special name** for a city.

Try it out!

On the map on the opposite page, draw where the Monster Gang's school could be. Write a **special name** for the school.

Blip the Blop

Read with your teacher.

Blip the Blop lives in Mush Mush Swamp.

Blip's job is to be mean and nasty. For most of the week, Blip is very good at his job.

On Monday he scares Tim Taddy.

On Tuesday Blip frightens Danny Duck.

On Wednesday he alarms Magda Moorhen.

On Thursday Blip shocks Pam Possum.

But on Friday when Blip startles himself ...

... he makes Tim, Danny, Magda and Pam laugh all day long on Saturday and Sunday!

Do you remember?

Some words are **proper nouns** (special names). They begin with a capital letter.

The days of the week are **proper nouns**. They must begin with a capital letter.

1 Use the clues to write **proper nouns** (special names) from the story about Blip.

a My job is to be scary and shocking. B ________ the B ________

b I am frightened on Tuesday. D ________ D ________

c Monday is my day to be scared. T ________ T ________

d I am alarmed on Wednesday. M ________ M ________

e I am shocked on Thursday. P ________ P ________

f I am startled on Friday. B ________ the B ________

2 Where does Blip the Blop live? ________________

Try it out!

Finish these **proper nouns** for the days of the week.

Monday, T ________________, ________________

________________, ________________

________________, ________________

The Monsters play Hidey

Read with your teacher.

The Monsters are playing.
They are going to play Hidey.

Em is IT. She has to look and chase.

Trang hid behind the flagpole.
He got caught.

Ali hid with Cara.
He got caught.

Max and Sami hid under a table. They got caught too!

Cara reached Home. She is the winner!

OXFORD UNIVERSITY PRESS

Instead of naming words, we sometimes use other words for people and things. These are called pronouns.

Read the words in this box.

Use words from the box to complete these sentences.

We	I	you	They
he	she	mine	

1 The Monsters are going to play a game. ___________ are going to play Hidey.

2 Trang hid behind the flagpole but ___________ got caught.

3 When Cara asked Max and Sami where they hid, they said, "________________ hid under a table."

4 When Em saw Ali, she said, "_________ can see you!"

5 When Em could not find Cara, she said, "Cara, where are ___________ ?"

6 Cara said to Ali, "This hiding place is ___________ !"

7 Em was IT, so ___________ had to look and chase.

We, **I**, **you**, **they**, **he**, **she** and **mine** are other words for people and things.

Try it out!

Can you write a sentence with more than one of these words in it?

we   I   you   they   he   she   mine

____

____

Nursery rhymes

Read with your teacher.

Davy Davy Dumpling

Davy Davy Dumpling
Boil Davy Davy Dumpling in a pot;
Sugar Davy Davy Dumpling
and butter Davy Davy Dumpling
And eat Davy Davy Dumpling
while Davy Davy Dumpling's hot!

Jack Spratt

Jack Spratt could eat no fat,
His wife could eat no lean;
And so between Jack Spratt and
Jack Spratt's wife both, you see,
Jack Spratt and Jack Spratt's wife
licked the platter clean.

When the poems are read out, they do not sound very good because the same nouns (naming words) have been used over and over.

Sometimes, instead of using nouns over and over again, it is better to use other words for people and things. These are called pronouns.

Use the short words from the boxes to fill the gaps.

him him he's him him

1 Davy Davy Dumpling,

Boil ____________ in a pot;

Sugar ____________ and butter ____________ .

And eat ____________ while ____________ hot!

They them

2 Jack Spratt could eat no fat,

His wife could eat no lean;

And so between ____________ both, you see,

____________ licked the platter clean.

Try it out!

Can you finish these sentences using words from the box?

a The book belongs to me. It is ____________.

b That bag belongs to Jenny. It is ____________.

c That pen belongs to Dad. It is ____________.

hers
mine
his

How the birds got their colours

Read with your teacher.

This is the story of how the birds got their colours.

Long, long ago – in the Dreamtime – when the land and the animals were being made, all of the birds were black – all one colour. Till one day a little dove flew around looking for food.

He flew down to the ground to catch a big, juicy grub.

But instead, he landed right on a sharp stick!

It pierced his little foot and made him very sick.

For days, he lay on the ground in pain. His foot swelled up.
He was dying!

All his mates gathered around to see how they could help. All except Crow. He just wandered around with his hands behind his back.

Suddenly, the parrot rushed forward – and, with her sharp beak, burst the little dove's swollen foot!

Colour splashed out all over the parrot.

Red and green and blue ran down her chest, wings and tail.

It splashed out all over the other birds.

Some got red, some brown, some blue, some yellow.

Some got spots. Some got stripes.
All got colours.

All except Crow, who was standing away from the others. Crow got no colour at all!

So that's how the birds got their colours.

Mary Albert of the Bardi people

OXFORD UNIVERSITY PRESS

Do you remember?

Nouns are used to name people, places and things.

1 Use the clues to help you finish these nouns from the story.

a Long, long ago in the D ______________ ...

b A little d ______________ flew around looking for food.

c Colour splashed out all over the p ______________ .

d Red, green and blue ran down her ch_____, w_____ and t_____.

2 Find these story words that tell you there is more than one (plural nouns).

a stripe ____________________

b spot ____________________

c colour ____________________

d mate ____________________

e wing ____________________

f bird ____________________

3 Rewrite this sentence by changing the repeated proper noun to a pronoun. Use the story to help you.

Crow got no colour at all because Crow was standing away from the others.

____

____

Try it out!

Choose an Australian animal you like.

- On a piece of paper, draw a picture of your animal.
- Label your picture with at least five nouns that tell us about your animal. Think about what your animal looks like, where it lives and what it eats.

Use your imagination and have fun!

Topic 1: Test your grammar

Nouns and pronouns

1 Shade the bubble below the **noun** (naming word).

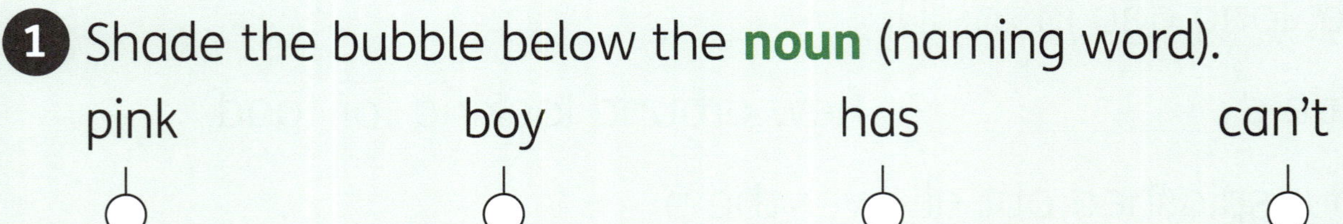

2 Shade the bubble below the **noun** (naming word) that matches this picture.

3 Shade the bubble below the **proper noun** (special name) for a person.

4 Shade the bubble below the **pronoun** (or other word) for **Jack** that could be used to fill the gap.

Jack wanted to visit Monster Town. ________ took a map with him.

She | They | He | We

5 Look at the pictures and then finish the sentences using words from the box.

He
mine
you
We
She

a ______________ are the Monster Gang.

b This is Max. ______________ likes to read.

c Here is Em. ______________ has a flag.
"This flag is ______________," says Em.

d "I can see ______________ behind the tree," said Trang.

6 Circle the words that show more than one.

trees monster birds maps flower

How am I doing? **Colour the boxes if you understand.**

Nouns are naming words. ☐

Proper nouns are special names. ☐

We, *I*, *you*, *they*, *he*, *she* and *mine* are pronouns (other words for people or things). ☐

Topic 2: Adjectives

Learning intention

We are learning to use adjectives to describe characteristics and add interesting descriptions in our writing.

Unit 2.1 Some words tell us about other words

The race

Ready, set, GO!

START

A **slow** car

An **old** car

A **sleepy** car

A **broken** car

A **fast** car

FINISH

Who do you think won the race?

____

Some words tell us more about nouns.
a ***big*** tree, a ***green*** leaf, a ***pretty*** flower
Big, ***green*** and ***pretty*** tell us more about a tree, a leaf and a flower.

1 Write the car number.

a Ali has a **slow** car. ______

b Trang's car is **fast**. ______

c Em has an **old** car. ______

d Max's car is **broken**. ______

e Cara has a **sleepy** car. ______

Use words that tell us more about nouns to make your sentences more interesting.

2 Write the five words from above that tell us more about the cars.

____

____

3 Some words can tell us more about the cars in the race. Fill in the blanks with the correct colour.

yellow purple blue green red

a Ali has a __________ car.

b Trang has a __________ car.

c Em has a __________ car.

d Max has a __________ car.

e Cara has a __________ car.

Try it out!

On a piece of paper, write some words that **tell us more about** what these animals are like.

a a tiger

b an elephant

c a shark

Monster mates

Tam has a **tall**, **thin**, **pink** pet.

Pat has a **big**, **fat**, **yellow** pot.

Dot is a **sad**, **sick**, **blue** monster.

Mot is a **slow**, **sleepy**, **purple** monster.

Tom has a **long**, **angry**, **red** face.

Mit is a **wet**, **sloppy**, **green** monster.

Some words tell us more about (describe) other words.

a ***red*** car, a ***clever*** student, a ***little*** cat, a ***round*** house, ***seven*** children

Red, ***clever***, ***little***, ***round*** and ***seven*** describe the car, the student, the cat, the house and the children.

1 Write the words that tell us more about:

a Tam's pet t________ t________ p________

b Pat's pot b________ f________ y________

c Dot the Monster s________ s________ b________

d Mot the Monster s________ s________ p________

e Tom's face l________ a________ r________

f Mit the Monster w________ s________ g________

2 Colour in the monsters on the page opposite, using the colours in the description.

Colour Tam's tall, thin pet.

Colour Pat's big, fat pot.

Colour sad and sick Dot.

Colour slow and sleepy Mot.

Colour Tom's long, angry face.

Colour wet and sloppy Mit.

Words that **tell us more about** (**describe**) naming words are called **adjectives**.

Try it out!

Circle the words in this sentence that **describe** the monster.

The huge monster was grey and hairy.

Ali's cubby

Read with your teacher.

Ali is making a cubby. First he hammers some strong, thick beams.

On the beams, Ali nails long, flat boards for the walls.

Next Ali puts down a smooth wooden floor.

Then he cuts out a small, square window.

When he has finished, Ali sits in a soft chair.

But here come some big, black clouds and …

Ali forgot to put a safe and snug roof on his cubby!

Do you remember?

Adjectives tell us more about (describe) other words. They describe the size, shape, colour, number, feelings and appearance of people, places and things.

a ***black*** coat, a ***happy*** face, a ***fluffy*** kitten, ***many*** people

Black, ***happy***, ***fluffy*** and ***many*** are adjectives. They describe a coat, a face, a kitten and some people.

1 Read the story about Ali. Add adjectives (describing words) to finish these sentences.

a The beams are s________________ and t________________ .

b The walls are made of l______________, f______________ boards.

c The floor is s________________ and w________________ .

d The window is s________________ and s________________ .

e The clouds are b________________ and b________________ .

2 Draw a line to the matching event.

First,	Ali puts down a smooth wooden floor.
Next,	Ali sits in a soft chair.
Then,	he hammers some strong, thick beams.
After he has finished,	he cuts out a small, square window.

Try it out!

Write **adjectives** that describe these faces.

____________ ____________ ____________ ____________

Lunar New Year

福

Read with your teacher.

It is time to celebrate!

There will be:

- colourful costumes
- dazzling fireworks to scare away bad luck
- loud music and lively dances
- busy markets selling yummy food
- glowing lanterns!

There may be red envelopes with money inside for lucky children.

There will be a grand parade with a fierce but friendly dragon to bring good luck!

Do you remember?

Adjectives are describing words. They tell us more about nouns.

1 Use the story to help you write the correct adjective.

a The costumes will be c____________________.

b The fireworks will be d____________________.

c The food will be y____________________.

d There may be r__________ envelopes with money.

e The children will be l____________________.

2 Draw lines to match the adjectives (describing words) with the words they tell us more about.

glowing	parade
busy	lanterns
grand	markets
lively	music
loud	dances

Words that describe the size, shape, colour and number of nouns are called adjectives.

3 Which two words in the story describe the dragon?

____________________ ____________________

Try it out!

Look at the photo on the opposite page. Can you write **adjectives** to describe these words?

t-shirt ________________ teeth ________________

pole ________________ eyes ________________

Adjectives

1 Shade the bubble below the **adjective** (describing word).

The huge elephant swished her trunk.

2 Shade the bubble below the **adjective** (describing word).

The clown gave me a blue balloon.

3 Shade the bubble below the **adjective** (describing word).

"Fold the square paper in half," said Mr Dan.

4 Shade the bubble below the **adjective** (describing word).

Dad cut the cake into twelve slices.

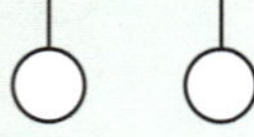

5 Circle the words that describe Pip and Gog.

Here is Monster Pip. Here is Monster Gog.

Monster Pip is:

brown spotty colourful dull shiny black unusual hairy

Monster Gog is:

orange spotty colourful dull shiny black unusual hairy

6 Choose words from the boxes above that do **not** describe Pip and Gog.

Monster Pip is not ________________________________.

Monster Gog is not ________________________________.

How am I doing? **Colour the boxes if you understand.**

Some words tell us more about other words. ☐

Adjectives tell us more about nouns. ☐

Adjectives are describing words. ☐

Topic 3: Verbs

Learning intention

We are learning to use verbs in our writing to tell us what is being done or what is happening. Verbs also tell us what has happened or what will happen.

Unit 3.1 Some words are doing words

Ziggy's robot

When Ziggy tells his robot, Benny, what to do, Benny does it.

Some words are called doing words because they tell us what is being done.
*I **eat** cake. We **drink** milk. They **lick** their ice creams.*
Eat, ***drink*** and ***lick*** tell us what is being done to the cake, milk and ice creams.

1 What did Benny do? Complete the missing words.

Benny w________ed. Benny r________n.

Benny ju________ed. Benny sk________ed.

Benny w________ed. Benny sl________t.

Doing words tell us what actions are being done or have been done.

2 Tick the things in this list that you can do.

walk ____	run ____	jump ____	climb ____
fly ____	sleep ____	swim ____	skip ____
work ____	try ____	drive ____	count ____
smile ____	knit ____	cook ____	play ____
sail ____	throw ____	wash ____	wink ____

Try it out!

Write what Benny can do.

____

____

____

The Monsters' Sports Day

Here is a picture of the Monsters at their Sports Day.

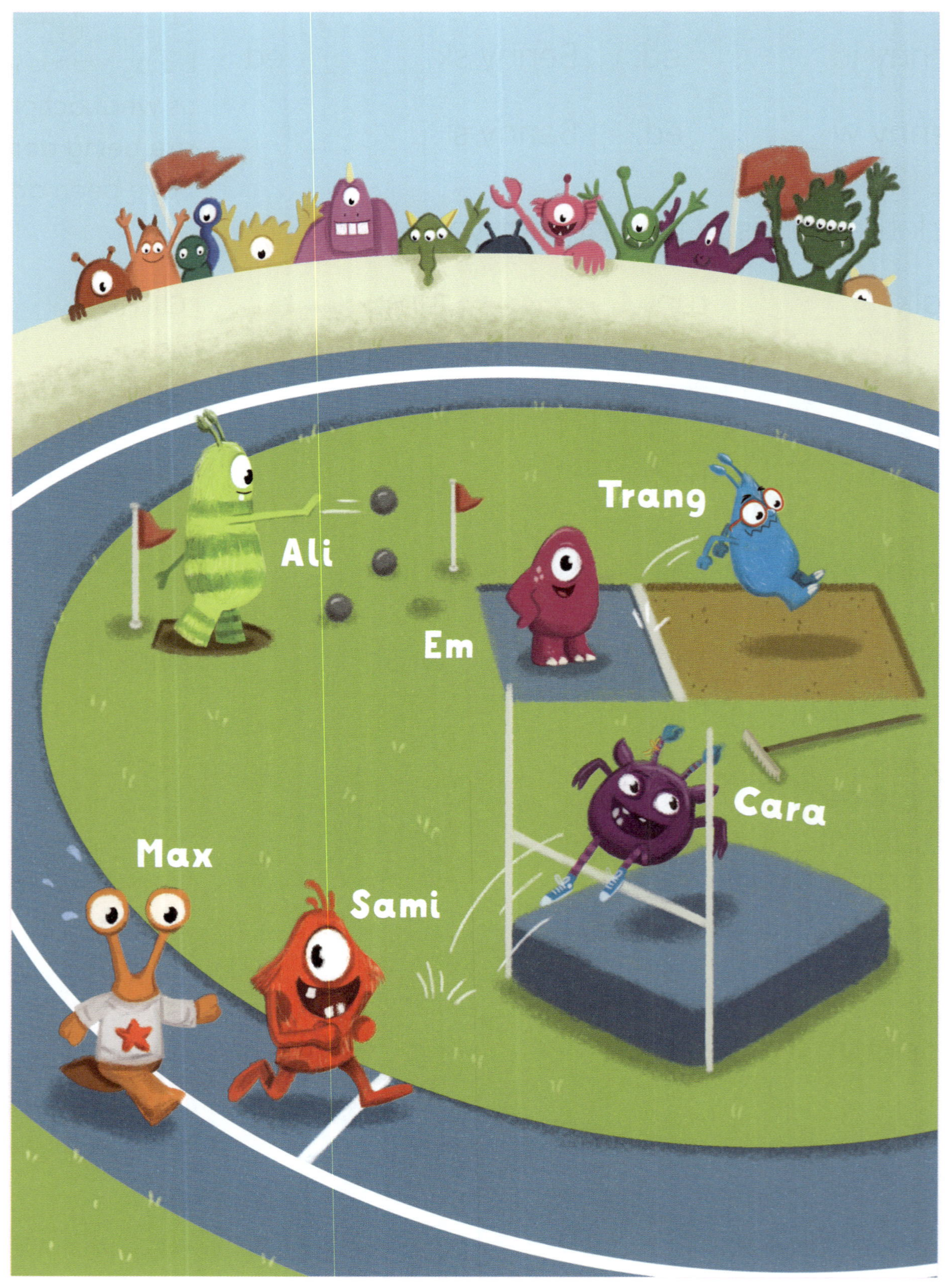

Some words are doing words. They tell us what is being done or what is happening.
Run, ***jump***, ***win*** and ***wait*** are all doing words.

1 Use the doing words from the box below to say what is happening at the Sports Day.

throws waits jumps
run wins leaps

Words that tell us what is being done are called **action verbs**.

a Ali ______________________ a shot put.

b Trang ______________________ into a sandpit.

c Cara ______________________ over a bar.

d Sami and Max ______________________ .

e Sami ______________________ the race with Max.

f Em ______________________ for her turn.

2 Draw lines to match each doing word group with the correct noun.

wash, scrub, dust, sweep	housework
slide, chase, catch, swing, kick	dinner
cook, fry, boil, stir, eat	playtime

Try it out!

Write three **doing words** telling what you might **do** at the swimming pool.

____

Pet Day

Do you remember the Monsters' pets?

My pet is
called Geeup.

My pet is
called Daddles.

My pet is
called Tabby.

My pet is
called Morton.

My pet is
called Octo.

My pet is
called Ruff.

Do you remember?

Some words are doing words. They tell us what is being done, what is happening or what will happen. They can also tell us what *was* being done or what *was* happening. Doing words are called verbs.

1 Choose the correct word and write it in the space.

a The ______________ was playing with Max.

b Tomorrow ______________ are taking our pets to the park.

c The ______________ were playing in the garden.

d The ______________ is spinning a web.

e The ______________ is Cara's pet.

cats/cat
we/I
pet/pets
spider/spiders
dog/dogs

2 When did it happen? Write verbs from the box in the "Before" or "Now" column.

jumped run crawled creep slide wriggled
fly slithered squirm leapt flap fluttered

Before (past)		Now (present)	
______________	______________	______________	______________
______________	______________	______________	______________
______________	______________	______________	______________

Try it out!

Can you write the names of animals that might make these sounds?

______________s roar, ______________s neigh, ______________s squawk

______________s hiss, ______________s bellow, ______________s buzz

Let's make naan

Read with your teacher.

Naan is a flatbread that comes from India.

Here is an easy way to make naan.

You will need:

- $1\frac{1}{2}$ cups of plain yoghurt
- 2 tablespoons of oil
- $2\frac{1}{2}$ cups of self-raising flour

What to do:

1. *Mix* together the yoghurt, oil and flour in a bowl to make the dough.
2. *Break* the dough into 16 pieces.
3. *Roll* the pieces into circles.
4. *Press* each piece until it is flat.
5. Ask an adult to *heat* a pan until it is hot.
6. *Toss* the flatbread dough into the pan.
7. *Cook* until the flatbread dough bubbles.
8. *Flip* the flatbread dough.
9. *Cook* until the naan is golden.
10. *Eat* your naan with your favourite sauce, dip or curry.

Verbs can also tell us about things that will happen later. We can use the words "will" or "going to" to talk about something that we plan to do.

For example: *I will play with my friends tomorrow.*
She is going to read a book tonight.

1 Use verbs from the recipe for naan to fill the gaps in these sentences.

a ______________________ together the yoghurt, oil and flour to make the dough.

b ______________________ each piece until it is flat.

c ______________________ a pan until it is hot.

d ______________________ the flatbread dough into the pan.

e ______________________ the breads until they are golden.

2 Write verbs from the box to finish these sentences.

wash   eat   cut   dip

a You can ______________ an apple in half with a knife.

b Here is some sauce to ______________ your naan into.

c After cooking you should ______________ your dishes.

d When you ______________ your naan it will taste yummy.

Try it out!

Draw lines to match.

eat	flew
feel	ate
fly	felt

sleep	ran
throw	slept
run	threw

Topic 3: Test your grammar

Verbs

1 Shade the bubble below the **verb** (doing word).

boy ○ robot ○ walk ○ desk ○

2 Shade the bubble below the word that tells what **action** is being done in the picture.

fish ○ snorkelling ○

mask ○ seaweed ○

3 Shade the bubble below the **verb** that completes the sentence.

Sami ____________________ to the shop and back.

feet ○ ran ○ legs ○ runned ○

4 Shade the bubble below the **verb** in this sentence.

Ruff barks loudly at the front gate.

○ ○ ○ ○

5 Shade the bubble below the **verb** that completes the sentence.

Esther __________ go to the movies with her family tonight.

have ○ wants ○ will ○ haven't ○

6 Draw and write three **actions** that you can do with a ball.

___________ ___________ ___________

7 Draw lines to match these things with what they do.

The wind	flies.
A baby	jumps.
A kangaroo	rings.
A bell	blows.
A runner	nips.
A jet	runs.
A crab	smiles.

How am I doing? **Colour the boxes if you understand.**

Verbs are doing words. ☐

Verbs tell us what has happened, what is happening or what will happen. ☐

Topic 4: Adverbs and phrases

Learning intention

We are learning to use adverbs and adverbial phrases to tell us when, where and how things happen in an interesting way in our writing.

Unit 4.1 "When" words

When did that happen?

Cara had no hair yesterday.

Today she has some hair.

Tomorrow Cara will have lots of hair!

Sami climbed into a box before.

Sami is hiding in the box now.

Sami will jump out and scare Em and Ali later.

Some words tell us **when** something happened.

Words that tell us **when** something happened are called **adverbs**.

1 Use the page opposite to help you finish these sentences.

a ______________________ Sami is hiding in the box.

b Cara will have lots of hair ______________________ .

c ______________________ Cara had no hair.

d Sami will jump out and scare Em and Ali ______________________ .

e ______________________ Cara has some hair.

f ______________________ Sami climbed into the box.

2 Put the above sentences in the right time order for Cara and Sami.

Cara: ______________________

____

____

Sami: ______________________

____

____

Try it out!

Finish these sentences about something you have done, something you are doing and something you will do.

a **Yesterday** I ______________________ .

b I am ______________________ **now**.

c I will ______________________ **later**.

Waiter! Waiter!

Anton the waiter serves food here.

Anton the waiter serves drinks there.

Tabby the cat sleeps here.

Tabby the cat sleeps there.

Sometimes ...

... food and drinks go everywhere!

Some words tell us **where** something happened.

1 Read "Waiter! Waiter!". Use **where** words from the story to answer these questions.

a Where does Anton serve food? ______________________

b Where does Anton serve drinks? ______________________

c Where does Tabby sleep? ________________ and ________________

d When Anton trips over Tabby, where do the food and drinks go? ______________________

2 Use **where** words from the box to complete these sentences.

> Words that tell us **where** something happened are called **adverbs**.

inside	outside	up	down

a The bird flew ____________________ into the treetops.

b The skateboard rolled ____________________ the hill.

c When the rain started, we ran ____________________ .

d When the Sun came out, we walked ____________________ .

Try it out!

Use the **where** word below in a sentence of your own:

(behind) ____

____

____

In the jungle

If we creep silently into the jungle and listen and look carefully, we might see and hear a scene like the one in this picture.

Some words tell us how something has happened, is happening or will happen.

Use the picture on the opposite page to help you write how words from the box to complete these sentences.

gently	silently	heavily	quickly
loudly	slowly	noisily	peacefully

1 The snail crawled ______________________.

2 The lion roared ______________________.

3 The elephant stomped ______________________.

4 The bear slept ______________________.

5 The monkeys chattered ______________________.

6 The cheetah ran ______________________.

7 The mouse squeaked ______________________.

8 The gorilla rocked her baby ______________________.

9 The snake slithered ______________________.

Words that tell us **how** something happened are called **adverbs.**

Try it out!

How must you creep into the jungle to see a scene like the one opposite?

____

____

Phrases

1 Draw:

a Humpty **on the wall.**

b the cow jumping **over the Moon.**

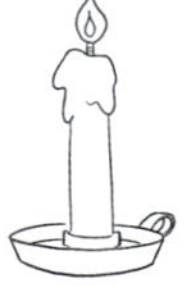

c Jack jumping **over the candlestick.**

d Jack going **up the hill.**

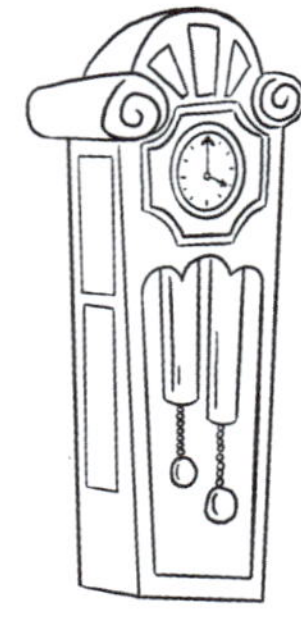

e the mouse running **up the clock.**

f a little star twinkling like a diamond **in the sky.**

2 Look at this picture of a playground.

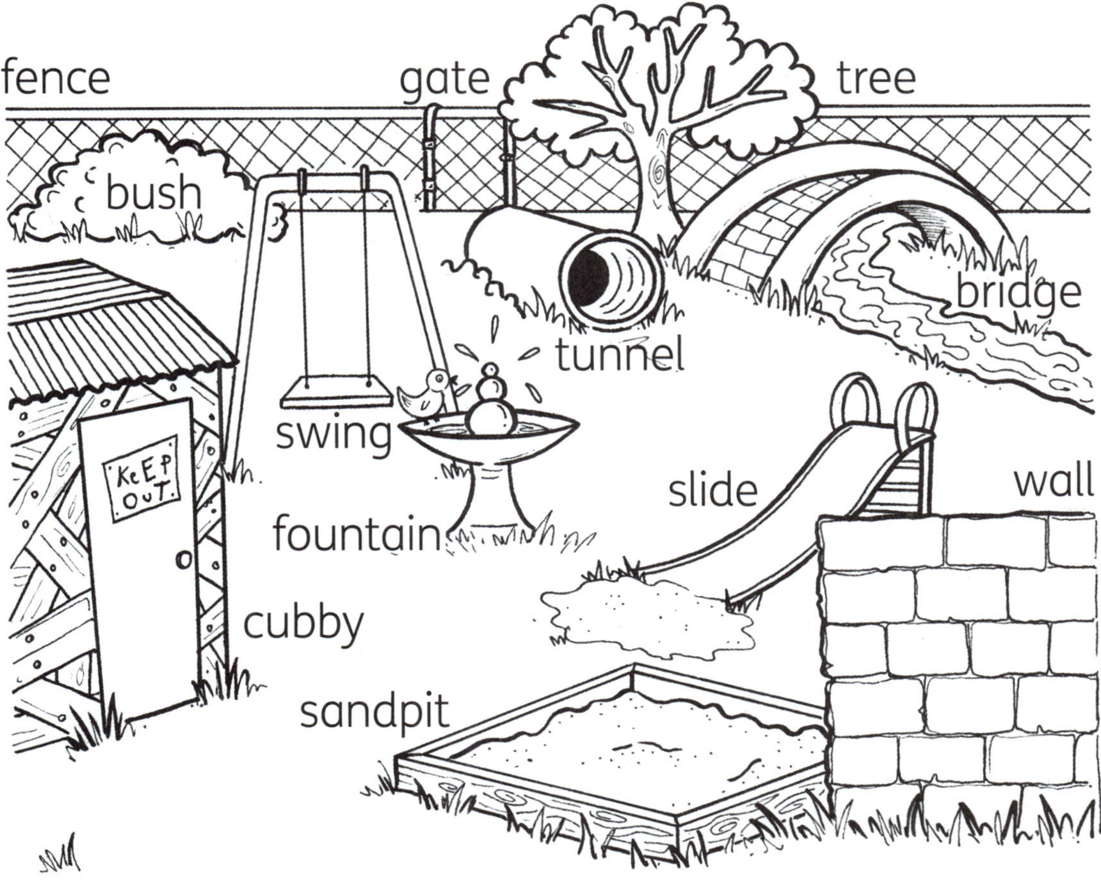

If the **fountain** is HOME, write some good places to hide in a game of Hidey. Colour in the places you choose.

a in the ______________________ **b** behind the ______________________

c on the ______________________ **d** under the ______________________

e up the ______________________ **f** near the ______________________

Try it out!

Twinkle, Twinkle, Little Star

Draw an arrow to match up the correct phrases.

When	"Up above the world so high"
Where	"Like a diamond in the sky"
How	"In the night"

Monsters at play

Do you remember the Monsters? Here they are at play.

Do you remember?

Words that tell us when, where or how things are happening are called adverbs.

Phrases are groups of words telling when, where or how something is happening.

Use adverbs or phrases from the box to finish the sentences about the Monsters at play.

on a chair	behind the box	quickly
loudly	quietly	inside the box

1. Cara is running ______________________ to catch Max.
2. Sami is hiding ______________________.
3. Trang is snoring ______________________.
4. Em is hiding ______________________.
5. Ali is sitting ______________________ reading a book.

Try it out!

Write sentences of your own to finish these:

a Last week I ______________________.

b Today I ______________________.

c Next year I ______________________.

Topic 4: Test your grammar

Adverbs and phrases

1. Shade the bubble below the word that tells **when** something happened.

box	some	early	walk
○	○	○	○

2. Shade the bubble below the word that tells **where** something happened.

outside	slowly	today	now
○	○	○	○

3. Shade the bubble below the word that tells **how** something happened.

yesterday	quickly	everywhere	Moon
○	○	○	○

4. Write a group of words to tell **where** Cara and Em are in the picture.

Cara and Em are ________________________________.

5 Write **adverbs** from the box telling when, where or how to finish these sentences about the pictures.

quickly	far	near
Today	anywhere	hard

a Ali is ______________________ (where) but Sami is ______________________ (where).

b (When) ______________________ it is hot so Max is wearing a hat.

c Em rode her skateboard ______________________ (how) past Sami.

d Trang is pushing ______________________ (how) but the log won't move ______________________ (where).

How am I doing?

Colour the boxes if you understand.

Adverbs tell us when, where and how things happen. ☐

Phrases are groups of words that tell us when, where and how things happen. ☐

Topic 5: Text cohesion and language devices

Learning intention

We are learning to use rhyme, repetition and alliteration to make our writing interesting.

Unit 5.1 **Repeating can make understanding easier**

Leon loves to race

1 Leon loves to run.
It is so much fun!

2 His legs are fast – not many can get past.

3 Leon loves to run.
It is so much fun!

The wind in his face and the great pace...

4 ...bring a smile to his face, as he loves to race.

5 As Leon does laps, Tim and Lin give high-five claps.

6 Leon wins the race!
Leon loves to race!

OXFORD UNIVERSITY PRESS

Some words are repeated to make understanding easier.

Use the story on the opposite page to help answer the questions.

1 Who is the story mainly about?

____

2 In the story, how many times has the author repeated:

a the name *Leon*? ______________________________

b the words *race* and *run*? ______________________________

3 Find a rhyming word in the story for each word below.

a fast ______________ **b** laps ______________

c face ______________ **d** fun ______________

4 What does Leon love to do? ______________________________

5 Word hunt: Find and circle the following words in the story.

fun fast face much so to

Try it out!

Read the story again. Find **words that mean the same as** these words.

a enjoyable ______________________________

b quick ______________________________

c grin ______________________________

Under the sea

Read with your teacher.

Let's dive!
There are jellyfish, catfish,
angelfish and clownfish too!

Here is a beautiful coral reef
with many colourful fish
swimming around it.

Now we have reached the sandy
bottom of the sea.
There goes a crab.
He wants to hide under a rock.

Here comes an octopus with
eight long arms.
We should keep an eye out
for hungry sharks.

It's time to swim back up to the
surface. If we are lucky we might see
a dolphin playing on the wave crests.

Some words belong together because they are about the same subject.

1 Where might you see the creatures in the story on the opposite page? ______________________

2 Tick the names of things that best belong under the sea.

umbrella	☐	catfish	☐	crab	☐
train	☐	desk	☐	coral reef	☐
shark	☐	whale	☐	sunken ship	☐
seahorse	☐	shell	☐	piano	☐
diver	☐	sand	☐	fruit tree	☐

3 Draw lines to match each group of words with where they best belong.

tractor paddock barn hayshed	school
computer desk locker playground	zoo
tie pants skirt scarf coat	farm
gorilla elephant giraffe kangaroo	wardrobe

Try it out!

Write the names of some things that **belong** in a kitchen.

____

____

____

Six silly songs

Read with your teacher.

Humpty Sami sat on a wall
Humpty Sami had a great ...

Little Miss Em
sat on a tuffet,
Eating her curds
and whey;
When down
came a spider,
and sat down ...

Ali be nimble,
Ali be quick,
Ali jump over the ...

Otto's playing tennis.
The sky is blue above.
Olga's playing
tennis too.
I think the
score is ...

Six swaggering sailors
set sail on stormy seas.
Six seasick sailors said,
"Back to the seashore ...!"

Jojo juggles jam jars,
Juice is juggled by Jess,
Jimbo juggles jelly,
And Jed cleans up the ...!

Some words rhyme.

1 Can you finish the rhymes from the opposite page? Look at the picture for clues.

a Humpty Sami had a great ______________________.

b And sat down ______________________.

c Ali jump over the ______________________.

d I think the score is ______________________.

When two or more words in a row begin with the same sound, it is called alliteration (say *uh-lit-er-ay-shun*).

2 Use words from the box to finish these sentences to show alliteration.

jam juggled seas sail

a Six sailors set ____________ on stormy ____________.

b Jojo juggles ____________ jars.

c Juice is ____________ by Jess.

Try it out!

Can you finish these tongue twisters that show **alliteration**?

a See silly Sally shearing sixty ______________________.

b P ____________ P ____________ picked a peck of pickled peppers.

Topic 5: Test your grammar

Text cohesion and language devices

1 Shade the bubble below the word that is **repeated** in this sentence.

Some frogs live in rivers while other frogs prefer trees.

some  frogs  rivers 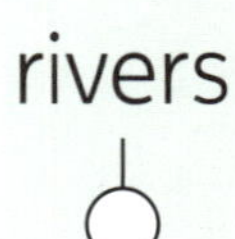 trees 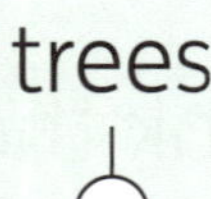

2 Shade the bubble below the best subject to match the group of words in the box.

dogs	cats	rabbits	birds

people ◯ zoo animals ◯ pets ◯ insects ◯

3 Shade the bubble below the word that would best complete this **rhyme**.

The clock on the wall said half-past eight.

I said to myself, "Oops! Now I'm ______________________ *!"*

nine 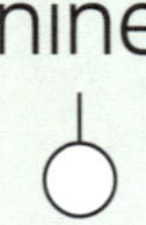 weight 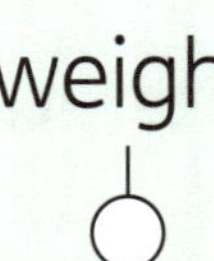 wait 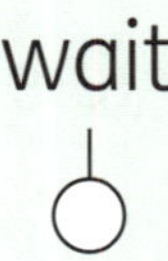 late ◯

4 Shade the bubble below the word that would best complete this sentence.

Seven silly sausages sailing seven ______________________.

seas ○ rivers ○ creeks ○ oceans ○

5 Complete this **rhyme**.

Noisy Neddy never naps.

Noni hogs the nest.

Mucky Marty makes a mess.

Maybe Mummy needs a ________________!

6 Complete your own **alliteration** sentences.

a Finn found five flying f ________________.

b Susie saw s ________________ s ________________.

c Bobby bought b ________________ b ________________.

How am I doing? **Colour the boxes if you understand.**

Sometimes words are repeated to make understanding easier. ☐

Some words belong together in groups. ☐

Some words rhyme. ☐

Topic 6: Sentences and punctuation

Learning intention

We are learning to write simple sentences, using who, what and where, to support our thinking; and we are learning that different types of sentences have different purposes (statements, questions and exclamations).

Unit 6.1 Who? Did what? Where?

The Monsters at the playground

Here is the playground where the Monsters play.

Some words in a sentence tell us who or what the sentence is about.
Some words in a sentence tell us what is happening.
Some words in a sentence tell us where something is happening.

The boy sat on the chair.

Who is the sentence about? ***The boy***
What did the boy do? ***sat***
Where did the boy sit? ***on the chair***

Here are the Monsters.

Em

Max

Sami

Ali

Trang

Cara

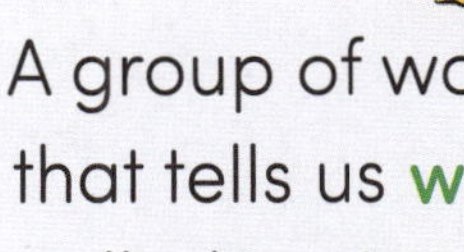

A group of words that tells us where is called a phrase.

Draw the Monsters in the playground on the opposite page. Who? Is doing what? Where?

1 Sami is playing on the flying fox.

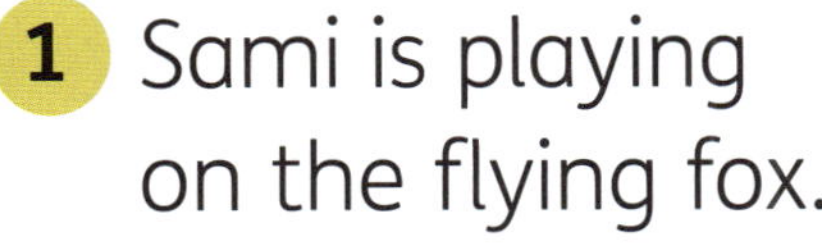

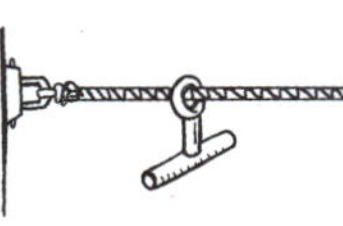

2 Em is hiding in the tunnel.

3 Trang is resting under the monkey bars.

4 Cara is sitting on the swing.

5 Ali is standing near the fountain.

6 Max is playing near the tyres.

Try it out!

a Draw yourself in the playground using one of these **phrases** to help you ...

near the roundabout
under the flying fox
on top of the tunnel
by a tree
on the monkey bars
between the two trees

b Write a **sentence** about your picture telling **Who? Did what? Where?**

____

____

The Monsters at home

A sentence is a group of words that makes sense.

A simple sentence tells us one main idea. For example:

Who or what?	*Is doing what?*	*Where?*
The dog	***is lying***	***under the table.***

1 Use the picture on the opposite page to help you write six simple sentences.

For example: *Trang is looking through the window.*

a Em is ______________________________.

b There is ______________________________.

c ______________________________.

d ______________________________.

e ______________________________.

f ______________________________.

Try it out!

Draw a circle around the group of words that makes a **sentence**.

Over the road	First you have to	It might rain tomorrow.
On Saturday	The pen is under	Car is

Unit 6.3 Simple sentences must make sense

When we grow up

Read with your teacher.

Trang wants to fly into space.

Cara wants to climb mountains.

Ali wants to invent a lollipop machine.

Em wants to be a movie star.

Max wants to sail around the world.

Sami wants to sleep in till late.

A simple sentence must make sense so the reader can understand it.

Tick the box next to each sentence.

A simple sentence tells a complete thought in a clear and direct way.

1
- ☐ Trang
- ☐ Trang wants to fly into space.
- ☐ in space
- ☐ to fly

2
- ☐ Em is going to be a movie star.
- ☐ Em movie star.
- ☐ Em going
- ☐ is going to be

3
- ☐ Max sail world will around to.
- ☐ Max will sail around the world.
- ☐ Max sail
- ☐ will sail

4
- ☐ Sami sleep late.
- ☐ Sami till late
- ☐ Sami sleep
- ☐ Sami will sleep in till late.

Try it out!

Tick the box next to each sentence.

- ☐ Cara wants to climb mountains.
- ☐ Cara wants to climb.
- ☐ Cara wants
- ☐ a lollipop machine
- ☐ Ali will invent a lollipop machine.
- ☐ Ali invents things.
- ☐ to climb
- ☐ when she grows up
- ☐ will invent
- ☐ Ali invents a

The Monsters and friends

Max, Cara and Em are good friends.

Blip, Tim, Danny, Magda and Pam live in Mush Mush Swamp.

Sami is reading a book called *Pet Ducks*.

Ali has called his cubby Ali's Pad.

The name of Ziggy's robot is Benny.

Trang and Morton live on Long Long Street.

OXFORD UNIVERSITY PRESS

Sometimes letters need to be written as capitals.

1 Read "The Monsters and friends". Circle all the capital letters.

2 Colour in the squares that have the capital letters.

A	a	B	b	C	c	D	d	E	e	F	f
G	g	H	h	I	i	J	j	K	k	L	l
M	m	N	n	O	o	P	p	Q	q	R	r
S	s	T	t	U	u	V	v	W	w	X	x
Y	y	Z	z								

Names begin with capital letters.

Special names of people, places and things are called **proper nouns**.

3 Write the names of these people, places or things so that there is a capital letter at the start of each name.

a max, cara, em ______________________________

b mush mush swamp ______________________________

c pet ducks (*a book name*) ______________________________

d ali's pad ______________________________

Try it out!

On a piece of paper, write the name of:

- one of your friends
- the state where you live
- a favourite book.

The mouse's tail

Read with your teacher.

The cat bit off the mouse's tail.

"Give me back my tail," said the mouse.

"First go to the cow and fetch me some milk," said the cat.

The mouse went to the cow.

"Please give me some milk," said the mouse.

"First go to the farmer and fetch me some hay," said the cow.

The mouse went to the farmer.

"Please give me some hay," said the mouse.

"First go to the butcher and fetch me some meat," said the farmer.

The mouse went to the butcher.

"Please give me some meat," said the mouse.

"First go to the baker and fetch me some bread," said the butcher.

The mouse went to the baker.

"Please give me some bread," said the mouse.

"If you promise not to nibble my cakes, I will give you some bread," said the baker.

"I promise," said the mouse, so the baker gave her some bread.

The mouse gave the butcher the bread.

The butcher gave the mouse some meat.

The mouse gave the farmer the meat.

The farmer gave the mouse some hay.

The mouse gave the cow the hay.

The cow gave the mouse some milk.

The mouse gave the cat the milk.

But the cat could not give the mouse her tail because she had eaten it.

That was the end of the mouse's tail and that is also the end of this tale!

OXFORD UNIVERSITY PRESS

Some sentences are statements that tell us something.

The car is red. ***My friend is Carla.*** ***I am going home now.***

A mark like this . ends a sentence.

The mark is called a full stop.

It tells us that the sentence has ended.

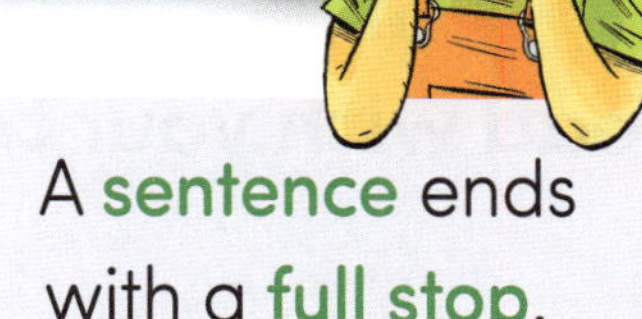

A sentence ends with a full stop.

Finish these sentences from "The mouse's tail".
Circle the full stop at the end of each sentence.

1 The cat bit ______________________.

2 The mouse went ______________________.

3 ______________________ to the farmer.

4 The mouse went ______________________.

5 ______________________ to the baker.

6 The mouse gave the butcher ______________________.

7 ______________________ the cow the hay.

Try it out!

Finish the **sentences** that answer these questions.

a What happened to the mouse's tail?

The cat ______________________

b Who did the mouse go to for some milk?

The mouse ______________________

Where's my mum?

Read with your teacher.

1

Lucy has lost her mother.

2

"Have you seen my mum?" Lucy asked the horse.

"No, I have not seen your mother. Have you asked the duck?" said the horse.

3

"Have you seen my mum?" Lucy asked the duck.

"Yes, I have seen your mother. She is in the shed," said the duck.

4

"Why are you in the shed?" Lucy asked her mother.

"It is time to take my wool off," said Lucy's mother.

"Does it hurt?" asked Lucy.

"No. Would you like to be shorn too?"

5

"No, thank you. I am too busy playing," said Lucy and off she ran into the paddock.

Some sentences ask something.

What is your name?	***Where is the cup?***	***How are you?***
When can I start?	***Is this your bag?***	***Who is that?***

Sentences that ask something end with this mark: ?

It is called a question mark. When you see this mark you will know that a question has ended.

1 Finish these questions from the story. Circle the question marks.

a Have you seen ______________________________?

b Why are ______________________________?

c Does ______________________________?

d Would you like ______________________________?

2 How many question marks can you count on the story page opposite? ____________________

3 Answer these questions.

a How many fingers are on one hand?

____

b Where do you live? ____________

____

____

c What is your favourite colour? ____________________

A sentence that asks something is called a question.

Try it out!

Draw lines to match the questions and answers.

Where do you live?	My name is Lucy.
What is your name?	My birthday is on Saturday.
When is your birthday?	I live in Victoria.

Help!

Help!

Eeek!

Oh no!

Look out!

No! Don't!

Help!
I'm telling!
Hey, stop that!
Take aim! Tap on! Fire!
Yikes!
Yeeow!

Some sentences are very short. They show feelings or shouting or orders.

Look out!	***Stop that!***	***Hey you!***	***Please let us in!***
Catch this!	***Ouch!***	***I'm over here!***	

A mark like this **!** is written at the end of a sentence that shows a feeling, or that someone is shouting or giving an order.

1 Write the missing marks after these sentences.

a Help **b** Look out

c Oh no **d** Hey, stop that

e Eeek **f** Take aim

Hey! A mark like this **!** means that someone has raised their voice. It is called an **exclamation mark**.

2 Choose a word from the box to write what you think is being said.

Help!
Goal!
Surprise!
Yikes!

Try it out!

Can you read these **sentences** aloud in three different ways?

- It's a bee.
- It's a bee!
- It's a bee?

Let's play footy!

These photos will help you answer the questions on the next page.

Photo A: Kiri takes them on!

Photo B: Can Meg break the tackle?

1 Use the boxes to help you rewrite each sentence correctly.

a P K . photo A shows kiri running with the ball

b W K ? will kiri kick the footy

c G K ! . “go kiri” they shouted

d O ! M . “oh no” meg is going to be tackled

e C S M ? can sally catch meg

Try it out!

Write your own question for each answer.

Q

A The players in Kiri’s team are wearing yellow socks.

Q

A She is playing rugby.

Topic 6: Test your grammar

Sentences and punctuation

1 Shade the bubble below the word in the sentence that tells **who** the sentence is about.

Max is playing on the tyres.

Max    playing ○   on 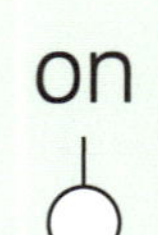   tyres ○

2 Shade the bubble below the words in the sentence that tell the **action** being done.

The girl is building a sandcastle at the beach.

girl ○   is building ○   a sandcastle ○   at the beach ○

3 Shade the bubble below the words in the sentence that tell **where** this happened.

The car stopped suddenly at the traffic lights.

The car ○   stopped ○   suddenly ○   at the traffic lights ○

4 Shade the bubble next to the sentence.

○ The blue balloon   ○ On the hill

○ I went to the shop.   ○ After dinner

5 On the lines, write what you think each Monster is saying.

HAPPY BIRTHDAY MAX!

____.

________________________!

____?

I am six.

____

____

How am I doing?

Colour the boxes if you understand.

A sentence tells us something. ☐

A sentence must make sense. ☐

Sentences begin with a capital letter. ☐

A sentence ends with a full stop. ☐

A question ends with a question mark. ☐

A mark like this **!** shows feelings, shouting or an order. ☐

Topic 7: Using grammar in texts

Learning intention

We are learning about informative, imaginative and persuasive texts and the type of language and punctuation we would find in them.

Unit 7.1 Using grammar in informative texts (procedure)

Berry-banana surprise!

A summer recipe

Read with your teacher.

Here's a great summer drink that's healthy and easy to make.

What you need:

1 banana

2 cups of strawberries

$\frac{1}{2}$ cup of fat-free natural yoghurt

$\frac{1}{2}$ cup of milk

a blender

Here's what to do:

1 Peel and chop the banana.

2 Remove the stems and leaves from the strawberries.

3 With an adult's help, place the fruit in the blender.

4 Blend for 30 seconds.

5 Add the milk and yoghurt.

6 Blend until smooth.

7 Pour your berry-banana surprise smoothie into a glass and ENJOY!

Recipes usually start by listing the names (nouns) of all the things we need.

1 Read the recipe. Which word in the box would name this group of words?

adjectives
verbs
adverbs
nouns

strawberries yoghurt blender

They are all ______________________.

Recipes need to be easy to read. They usually include steps, in order, with commands telling us what to do. ***Add the milk and yoghurt*** is a command. It tells us what to do.

2 Read the recipe. Write the first command telling what to do.

____

3 Write a command to give an order to a classmate.

____

4 Look at the coloured verbs (doing words) in each step of the recipe. In each command, where is the verb usually placed?

at the start ☐ in the middle ☐ at the end ☐

Try it out!

Circle the word groups below that give **commands**.

in the blender	into a glass	Add the yoghurt.
Here's a great	Rinse the strawberries.	Easy to make

My dog, Doug

I have a dog
and his name is Doug
and a digging dog is he.

Doug digs down deep
while I'm asleep
for a digging dog is he.

When Dad awakes
to the mess Doug makes
"You're a daggy dog!" says he.

But I love Doug
with the digging bug
and I think that Doug loves me!

AjW

Poems often use playful rhyming lines or rhyming words. For example, ***he*** and ***me*** rhyme.

1 Read "My dog, Doug". Use different colours to circle each pair of rhyming words.

2 Circle the words in each group that rhyme.

a	Doug	bug	dog	though	slug
b	leap	deep	sleep	green	deer
c	train	claim	name	blame	time

Alliteration (say *uh-lit-er-ay-shun*) is often used to make poems entertaining. Alliteration uses two or more words in a row, beginning with the same sound.

3 Which letter is used at the beginning of a lot of words in the poem about Doug? ____________________

4 Add the letter **d** to complete this line of alliteration from the poem.

___oug ___igs ___own ___eep.

Poems sometimes end with an exclamation mark to show feelings.

5 Add exclamation marks (!), where needed, to the sentences.

You're a daggy dog

What are you doing, Doug

Stop that, Doug

Doug loves me

Try it out!

Why do you think the poet (AjW) chose Doug as the **special name** (proper noun) for a dog that spends a lot of time digging holes?

____

Live music

Yummy food!
Delicious drinks!

Come and join us at the
FABULOUS

Barton School Fair

FREE pony rides on the school oval!

Are you brave enough to visit the haunted house?

Saturday 4 November
10 a.m. - 3 p.m.

Bop the Clown will make an appearance at 1 p.m.

Have fun in the jumping castle!

Lots of amazing stalls and races!

Ads (advertisements), such as the poster on the opposite page, often use exclamations to excite the reader and persuade them to do or buy something.

1 Read the poster for the Barton School Fair. Circle all the exclamations and exclamation marks (!) used to make the fair sound exciting.

2 Write the question from the poster that asks something about the Barton School Fair.

____

____

Nouns (naming words) are found in all texts. The nouns in the poster are all about the topic – the Barton School Fair.

3 Add nouns to the boxes below to name exciting things you might see at the Barton School Fair.

castle			

4 Proper nouns (special names) start with a capital letter. Use the clues below to write proper nouns from the poster.

a I am a funny entertainer. _______________

b I am the name of the fair. _______________

c I am a month. _______________

Try it out!

Look at the poster and write the **adjectives** (describing words) that are used to **describe** these.

_______________ drinks _______________ stalls _______________ pony rides

Topic 8: Extension and enrichment

Learning intention

We are learning about antonyms, synonyms, articles and joining words to make our writing interesting.

Unit 8.1 Some words can be opposites (antonyms)

Opposites

1 Match the opposites. Make each pair of words the same colour.

sad

hot

asleep

out

awake

night

happy

cold

up

day

in

down

Some words can have opposite meanings. They are called antonyms.
Here are some opposites ... ***big/small*** ***fast/slow*** ***start/finish*** ***hard/soft***

Finish the sentences.

2 This door is open.

Another word for **opposite** is **antonym**.

This door is ____________________ .

3 This switch is off.

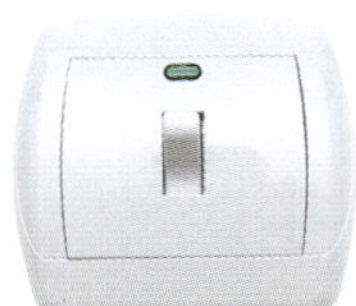

This switch is ____________________ .

4 This girl is at the top.

This girl is at the ____________________ .

5 This traffic light means stop.

This traffic light means ____________________ .

Try it out!

Finish the sentence with **opposites**.

What goes ____________________ must come ____________________ .

Words that mean the same

1 Match each group of words that mean the same (or nearly the same) by making them the same colour.

happy

wet

sprint

large

little

jolly

big

run

huge

small

damp

soggy

glad

jog

tiny

massive

Some words mean the **same** (**or nearly the same**) as other words. They are called **synonyms**.

Circle the word that does not belong in each group.

2

cup  mug  dish  glass

3

hat  boot  cap  helmet

4

shed  cabin  hut  slide

5

fast  slow  quick  speedy

Try it out!

Circle the word that does not belong in each group.

a cold cool icy hot

b little big small tiny

People in the community

A

I fly an aeroplane every day.

B

I help people when they are sick.

C

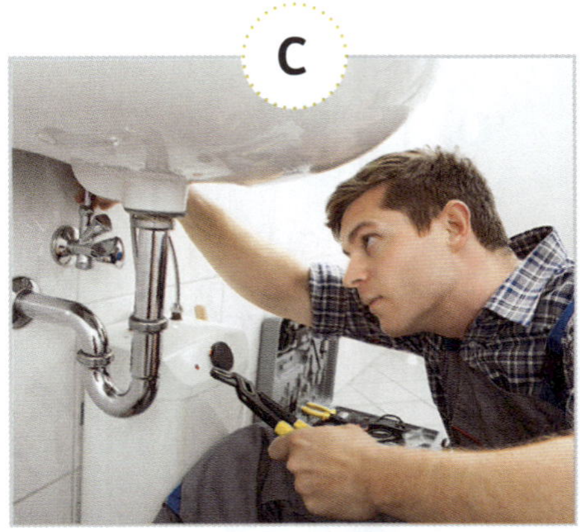

I fix water pipes when they burst.

D

I help to keep animals well.

E

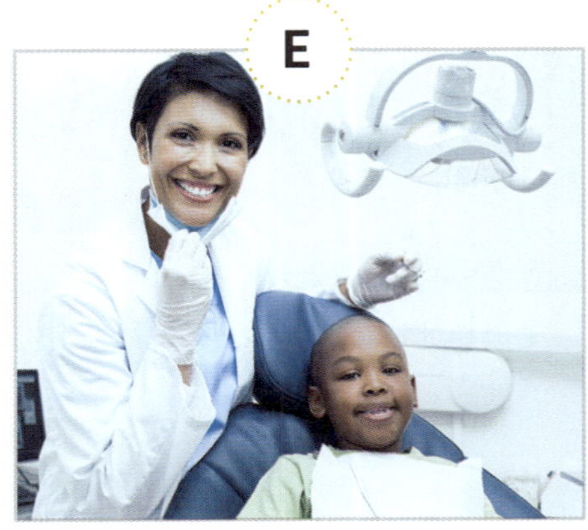

I look after your teeth.

F

I grow crops for food.

G

I write books.

H

I act in films or television shows.

I

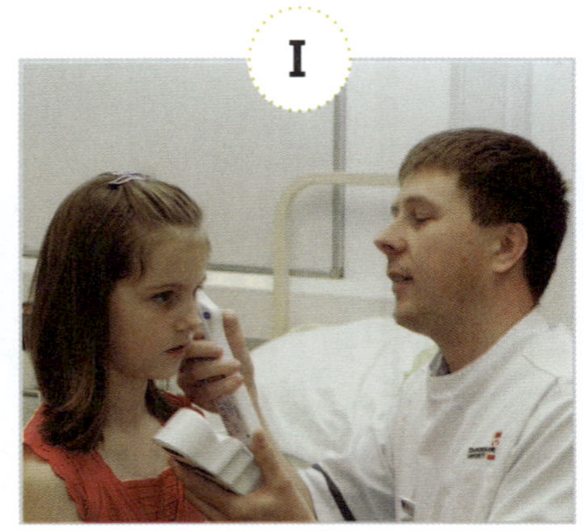

I look after sick people in hospital.

Nouns (naming words) often use ***a*** or ***an*** in front of the name: for example, ***a*** teacher, ***an*** astronaut, ***a*** vet.

The words ***a*** and ***an*** are called articles. We place the article ***an*** in front of most nouns that start with a vowel (a, e, i, o, u are vowels): ***an a****ctor,* ***an e****ngine driver,* ***an u****mpire.*

1 Match the job and picture clue with the people on the opposite page. Write the correct letter in the box.

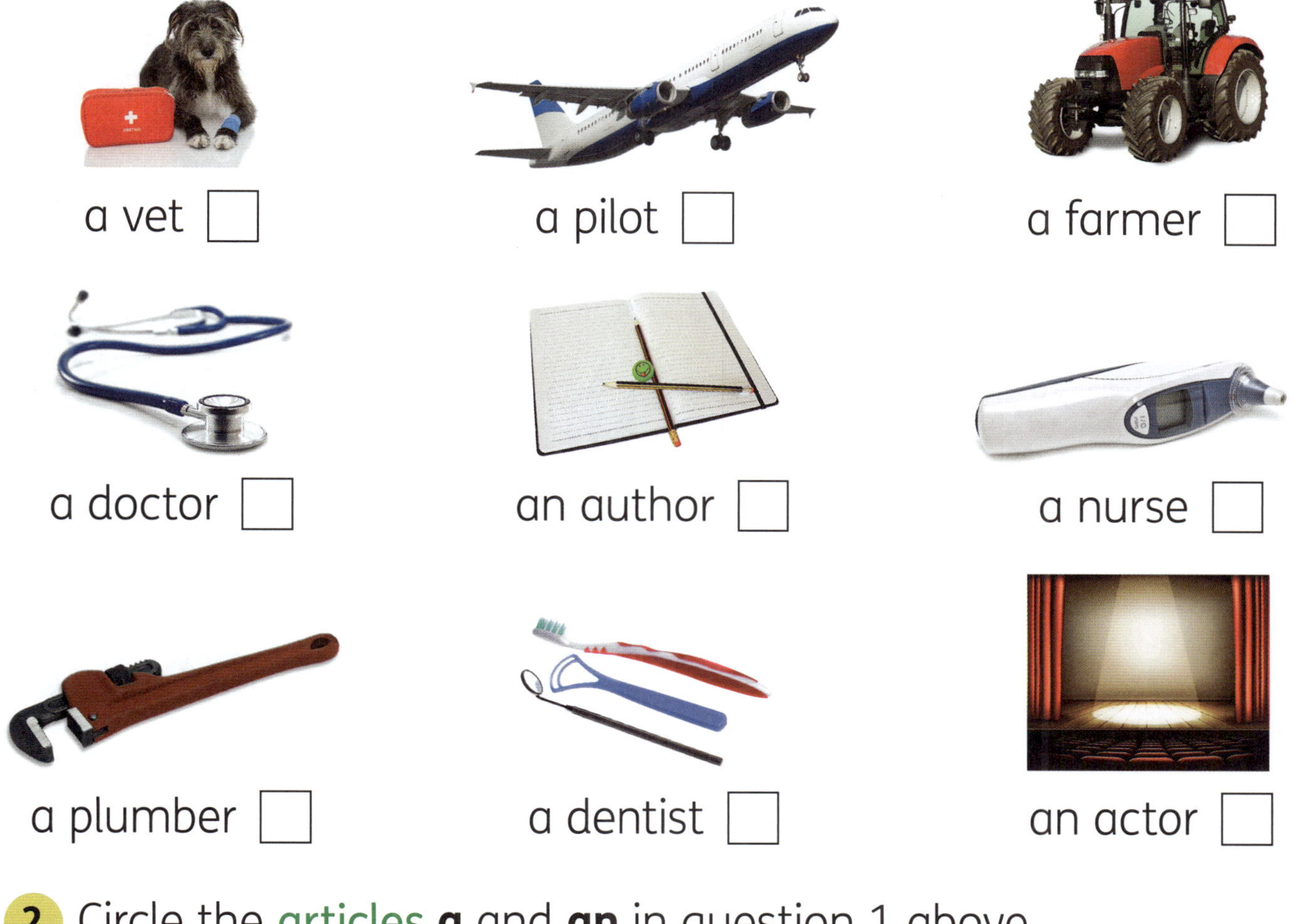

a vet ☐ a pilot ☐ a farmer ☐

a doctor ☐ an author ☐ a nurse ☐

a plumber ☐ a dentist ☐ an actor ☐

2 Circle the articles **a** and **an** in question 1 above.

3 When do we use the article **an**? ______________________________

____

Try it out!

Name a place where a nurse works. ______________________

What is something an author might write? ______________________

Who looks after people's teeth? ______________________

Spiders

Read with your teacher.

The spider is an arachnid.
Some spiders are dangerous.
A spider is not an insect.
The orb weaver spins a web.

The female redback is poisonous.

The female redback has a large, black body.

The Sydney funnel-web likes to hide.

We can join sentences together by adding ***and***, ***but*** or ***so***. These joining words are called conjunctions.

Use the sentences on the opposite page to make longer, more interesting sentences.

1. ______________________ and it has eight legs.
2. ______________________ so it can catch insects.
3. ______________________ and others are harmless.
4. ______________________ and she has a red stripe on her back.
5. ______________________ so shake your shoes before you put them on.
6. ______________________ but it does like to catch and eat insects.
7. ______________________ but the male is not dangerous.

Try it out!

Using **and**, **but** or **so**, write your own interesting **sentence** about spiders.

____

____

____

The ant and the grasshopper

Read with your teacher.

Once upon a time in a grassy meadow, there lived a grumpy ant named Andy and a sad grasshopper named Lily. Andy was grumpy because he was always busy working, while Lily loved playing her violin but was sad because she felt lonely.

One day, as Andy was carrying a crumb, he heard Lily's beautiful music. "Why are you sad, Lily?" he asked.
"I wish someone would listen to my music," Lily sighed.

Andy thought and said, "You play while I work. I'll take breaks to enjoy your music. We can help each other!" Lily's eyes lit up, and she agreed.

From then on, Lily played her violin while Andy worked, making his work lighter and her heart happier. Other insects joined in, and the meadow became a cheerful place.

Andy wasn't grumpy any more, and Lily wasn't sad. They had found the joy of sharing and became the best of friends, bringing music and happiness to everyone.

Grace Romano

Some words name people, places and things. They are called nouns.

1 Use nouns from the box to fill in the gaps.

crumb everyone meadow

a Once upon a time in a grassy ________________ ...

b One day, as Andy was carrying a ________________ ...

c Bringing music and happiness to ________________ ...

Some words describe people, places and things. They are called adjectives.

2 Find adjectives in the story that describe the following.

a Once, there lived a g________________ ant named Andy and a s________________ grasshopper named Lily.

b Lily's b________________ music ...

c The meadow became a ch ________________ place.

Some words tell us about action. They are called verbs.

became
played
worked
joined

3 Use verbs from the box to fill the gaps in these sentences.

From then on, Lily p________________ her violin while Andy w________________. Other insects j________________ in, and the meadow b________________ a cheerful place.

Try it out!

a On a piece of paper, write words from the story that mean the **opposite** to these words.

happy popular resting

b Find story words that mean **the same**, or nearly the same, as these words.

cranky unhappy lovely

Topics 7 and 8: Test your grammar

Opposites, synonyms and conjunctions

1. Shade the bubble below the word that is **opposite** to **long**.

high	short	little	heavy
○	○	○	○

2. Shade the bubble below the word that is **opposite** to **top**.

above	over	bottom	pot
○	○	○	○

3. Shade the bubble below the word that is **opposite** to **old**.

young	tall	thin	open
○	○	○	○

4. Shade the bubble below the word that means **the same as thin**.

narrow	wide	thick	bad
○	○	○	○

5. Shade the bubble below the word that means **the same as fast**.

slow	quick	small	cry
○	○	○	○

6. Shade the bubble below the word that means **the same as little**.

large	smell	small	big
○	○	○	○

7 Shade the bubble next to the word that would best **join** the two sentences to make one sentence.

A giraffe is tall. *A meerkat is short.*

○ or ○ but ○ so ○ for

8 Shade the bubble next to the word that would best **join** the two sentences to make one sentence.

An ant is an insect. *It has six legs.*

○ or ○ but ○ so ○ and

How am I doing? **Colour the boxes if you understand.**

Some words can have opposite meanings. ☐

Some words can have the same or nearly the same meaning. ☐

Some words can be used to join sentences together. ☐

Time to reflect

Colour each box when you can do the following things.

- ☐ **nouns** I can use naming words when I write sentences.
- ☐ **plural nouns** When there is more than one of something, I can add an **s** to the end of some nouns.
- ☐ **proper nouns** When I write the special names for people, places and things, I begin with a capital letter.
- ☐ **pronouns** I understand that words such as **we**, **I**, **you**, **they**, **he**, **she** and **mine** can be used for people and things.
- ☐ **adjectives** I can use describing words when I write sentences.
- ☐ **verbs** My sentences always contain a word or words telling what is being done or what is happening.
- ☐ **adverbs (when, where and how words)** I can use words that tell **when**, **where** and **how**.
- ☐ **phrases** When I write my sentences, I can use groups of words that tell when, where or how things are happening.
- ☐ **capital letters** I use a capital letter to begin a sentence and to begin a proper noun.
- ☐ **full stops** I use a full stop (**.**) to end a sentence.
- ☐ **question marks** I use a question mark (**?**) to end a question.
- ☐ **exclamation marks** I use an exclamation mark (**!**) to show that someone is using a raised voice.
- ☐ **synonyms** I can write words that mean the same (or nearly the same).
- ☐ **antonyms** I can write opposites.
- ☐ **joining words (conjunctions)** I can join sentences with words such as **and**, **but**, **so**.

Glossary

adjective	A word that describes or tells us more about other words (nouns). *fast, old, black, sleepy, angry*
adverb	A word that tells when, where or how. *today* (when), *here* (where), *quickly* (how)
alliteration	A group of words that begin with or contain the same sound. *seven silly sausages*
antonym	An opposite. *hot/cold, fast/slow, dry/wet, up/down*
article	The words *a* and *an*.
capital letter	An upper-case letter. *A B C D E F G H I J K L M N O P Q R S T U V W X Y Z*
conjunction	A word that can join two parts of a sentence. *and, but, so*
exclamation	A sentence that expresses a raised voice or strong feeling. *Look at that!*
exclamation mark	An exclamation mark (**!**) goes at the end of an exclamation. *Hello!*
full stop	The mark (.) that shows us where a sentence ends. *Max is hiding behind a tree.*
noun	A word that names people, places, animals, things, feelings or ideas. *girl, ball, beach, forest, table, horse, happiness*
phrase	A group of words that tells us how, when or where. *snoring loudly, it rained today, over the hill, under the bridge*
plural noun	When there is more than one of something, we add an **s** to the end of some nouns. *one dog, two dogs one hat, ten hats*
pronoun	A word that can take the place of people, places or things. *Penny is having a birthday. **She** is six today. (he, she, I, it, they, we, us, me)*

Glossary *continued*

proper noun	A special naming word for people, places and things. A proper noun always begins with a capital letter. *Cara, Mr Lewis, Australia, Baker Street, Easter*
punctuation	Special symbols or marks, such as a comma or full stop, that show a pause or break in a sentence.
question	A sentence that asks something. *Are you going to Maddy's party?*
question mark	A question mark (**?**) goes at the end of a question. *What is your name?*
rhyming words	Words that sound the same. *snow/flow, best/rest, dog/log*
sentence	A group of words, containing a verb, that makes sense. *The birds were sitting on the fence.*
statement	A sentence that states facts or gives opinions. *The horses ran around the paddock.*
synonym	A word that means the same or nearly the same as another word. *cry/weep, run/jog, big/large, unhappy/sad*
verb	A word that tells us what is happening or what is being done in a sentence. Verbs can also tell us what was happening or was being done, or what will happen or will be done. Verbs can be: **doing (**or **action) verbs**: *throw, sit* **relating verbs**: *am, is, are, was, were, has, have, had* **saying verbs**: *said, whispered* **thinking and feeling verbs**: *know, like*